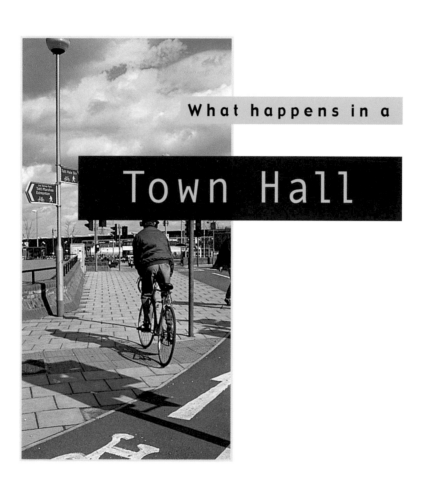

What happens in a

Town Hall

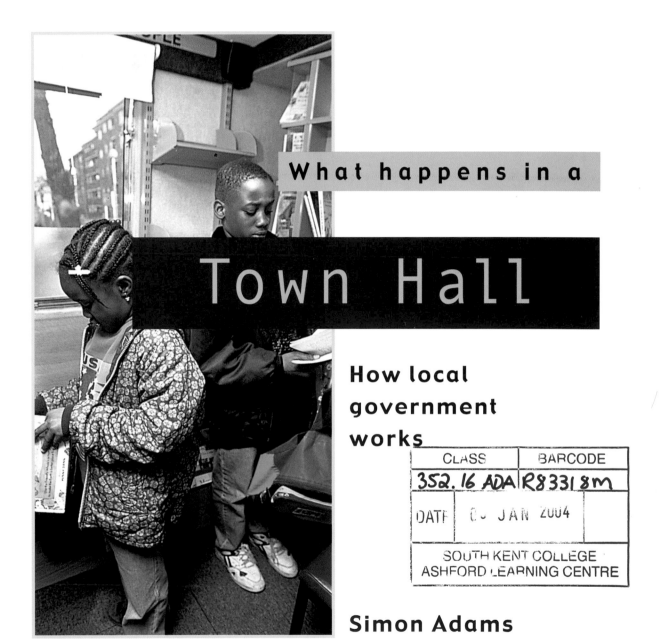

What happens in a

Town Hall

How local
government
works

Simon Adams

W
FRANKLIN WATTS
LONDON • SYDNEY

About the author
Simon Adams lives in South London and served as a councillor on Lambeth Council for six years. He was educated at the London School of Economics and Bristol University, and is a full-time writer of children's non-fiction books.

Key words
To help you find your way around this book, key words are printed in **bold**. You can find some of these words in the glossary on pages 30-31.

Illustrations Alastair Taylor/The Inkshed

Designer Magda Weldon
Editor Penny Clarke
Art Director Jonathan Hair
Editor-in-Chief John C. Miles

© 2000 Franklin Watts

First published in 2000
by Franklin Watts
96 Leonard Street
London
EC2A 4XD

Franklin Watts Australia
14 Mars Road
Lane Cove
NSW 2066

ISBN 0 7496 3761 7

Dewey classification: 352

Printed in Malaysia

Contents

Introduction

Walk into the centre of any town or city and you will find an impressive town hall. This is the headquarters of your local council. The people working in it have a huge impact on your daily life.

Local government – a brief history

Until the 19th century, **local government** in Britain was disorganised. Most towns had **councils** but their powers varied. Many basic services, such as street lighting, were run by separate bodies.

To sort this situation out, Parliament established **municipal corporations** for towns and cities in 1835, **county councils** in 1888-89, **rural district councils** in 1894 and **London boroughs** in 1899.

THE TOWN HALL is often a large and impressive old building located at the centre of a city or town.

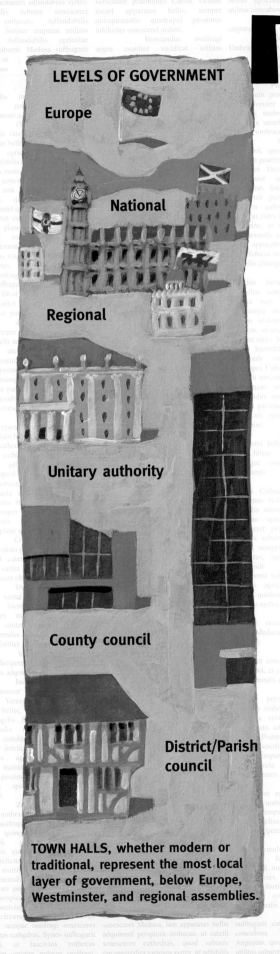

LEVELS OF GOVERNMENT

Europe

National

Regional

Unitary authority

County council

District/Parish council

TOWN HALLS, whether modern or traditional, represent the most local layer of government, below Europe, Westminster, and regional assemblies.

The twentieth century

During the twentieth century, the structure of local government continued to change as the population grew, particularly in cities and towns. In 1972-73 a two-level system was introduced across the country, with a top level of **counties** (called **regions** in Scotland) and a second, lower, level of **districts**. **Parish councils** created a third tier in some areas.

Today, that structure is fast disappearing. In the more rural areas of England, 34 **county councils** and 238 **district councils** survive, but the rest of the country is governed by 195 **unitary authorities**. Many of the unitary and district councils are called **boroughs** or **cities**. There are also about 10,000 **parish councils**, mostly in rural areas.

What do local authorities do?

Unitary authorities look after every aspect of **local government**, from education and social services to housing and planning. In more rural areas, **county councils** deal with strategic planning and services such as education and the fire service, while **district councils** look after local planning, street maintenance and amenities like rubbish collection.

Three layers of government

There are three layers of government in Britain: **national**, **regional** and **local**. The Parliament at Westminster is the top layer, governing the whole country. Below that is regional government: a Scottish parliament and Welsh and Northern Irish assemblies were set up in 1999, and a strategic authority established in London in 2000.

Local government is the most local layer of government in the UK. But its structure and functions are decided by Parliament, and it is from Parliament that local government gets all its powers and responsibilities.

Not sure what goes on in your local town hall? No idea about the role or purpose of local government? Then think about a typical day in your life, perhaps a weekday during term-time when you go to school.

SOME OF THE THINGS that your local council is **responsible for include traffic signs, street crossings, schools and parks.**

Into the street

Early in the morning you are woken up by the dustmen crashing bins around in the street. After breakfast you leave your home and walk along the pavement towards school. You cross the road on a pedestrian crossing, and watch cars crawling along the yellow lines until they find a space with a parking meter. There are street signs to tell you where you are, and a cleaner is hard at work getting rid of the litter.

The school day

Once at school, you sit through lots of lessons as your teachers try to make you learn something.

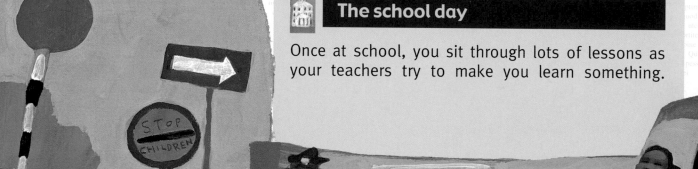

The visiting music teacher comes to take a singing lesson. You have a school dinner served by a school dinner lady, and during the afternoon you go to the swimming pool for a swimming lesson. Once school is over, you and your mates stop off in the local park. Then you head home, stopping off first at the library. You look in at your gran's to see if she is all right. Meals-on-wheels came today, so she had a nice lunch. Then you return home. It is getting dark now, and the street lights are coming on.

Just imagine...

Just a normal day, really, like any other day of the week. But imagine that day if there were no local government in your town. No pavements to walk on, or paved streets. No traffic lights and parking meters and yellow lines to control the traffic. No school or school lunch, no visiting music teacher or swimming lessons in the local pool. No local park or library, no social services for your gran, no street lights to light up the evenings. And those are just the things you can see – there are plenty of 'invisible' things, such as the drains!

Under control

Your local council runs education and social services, street cleaning and road building, traffic lights and street signs, food hygiene and environmental health, council housing and building control. It sets its own local laws, called **bylaws**, and runs the **elections** for councillors and MPs.

Local councils do so much that it is almost easier to say what they do not do. Defence, foreign affairs, taxation, social policy, law-making and transport policies are all looked after by the **national government** in London, while **regional governments** take care of affairs in Scotland, Wales and Northern Ireland. You might not notice your local council as much as the national government, but you couldn't live without it.

Look up your council's website on the Internet. You'll be amazed at its contents.

One of your local council's most important responsibilities is to look after the streets. Not just the road surfaces, but the right to park in them and the flow of traffic along them.

MANY OF THE THINGS you can see in this photograph are the responsibility of the local council.

Cars rule?

Fifty years ago there were very few cars on the road. Today, many families have at least one car. As a result, our towns and cities are very congested. Local councils ease congestion by setting up **controlled parking zones** (CPZs). To use these, drivers must have a permit or pay at a meter or machine. The council employs **traffic wardens** to enforce these schemes.

Controlling the car

The council can also control the flow and volume of traffic by introducing speed limits, road humps and other measures. It can make a street one-way. It also looks after traffic lights and pedestrian crossings.

If the council has enough money, it can build a new road, but most councils can only afford to maintain existing roads by mending pavements and potholes or by resurfacing.

The council also keeps the streets clean and well lit. It employs refuse collectors to empty dustbins, street cleaners to get rid of litter and makes sure the street lights work.

Next time you step out of your door, look around you. Almost everything you see is the result of action by your council.

Green streets

All these measures are intended to make the roads safer for both pedestrians and motorists by cutting down car use. Councils are now very aware that cars damage the **environment** and cause pollution. Some local councils therefore ban cars from town centres. They set up **cycle routes** and encourage people to cycle or walk, rather than drive.

A safer environment

Looking after the streets is only one aspect of the environment that the council controls. **Environmental health** inspectors visit restaurants and food shops, including supermarkets, to check they are clean and safe. They monitor **air quality** to measure pollution and take action against persistent polluters. They also get rid of rats and other vermin.

In addition, the council controls the hours pubs, clubs and restaurants can open, and makes sure late-night venues do not disturb local residents. **Noise patrols** seize noisy stereo equipment and stop late-night parties, as well as protecting people from noisy or nuisance neighbours.

Regulating building

Finally, the council can decide which **buildings** are put where. All decisions about the number, location and size of **new houses**, the building of **supermarkets** or **factories** and the conversion of old buildings for new uses are controlled by the council. This is to make sure that our towns are not overcrowded and that the streets we live in are not dominated by unsuitable buildings.

Our physical and natural environment is precious to all of us, and the council plays a major role in making sure that it is not damaged or destroyed.

Many people in Britain are poor or suffer from ill health. An increasing number are also old and infirm. Local councils play an important part in helping to care for these people.

Many vulnerable and ill people rely on the council to provide a roof over their heads and food and care during the day.

Council housing

A century ago many people in Britain lived in **slum housing**. Gradually, these old houses were swept away and vast **estates** were built, owned and run by local councils. Today these estates are being broken up: many tenants have bought their homes, while the ownership of some estates has passed to **housing associations** or **private landlords**.

Even so, councils still own and manage about one-fifth of all homes in Britain and continue to have a duty to house the homeless. Councils also offer homes to people on low incomes.

Social services

The provision of **social services** is not perhaps as well known as, say, education. But it takes a large part of a council's total budget and is one of the most important services it offers.

Helping children

Through its social services the council looks after two main groups of people. The first are **children** who are in need or at risk.

Social workers help families to stay together through a temporary crisis, but if a child's life is at risk from abuse or neglect, the council steps in and

LOCAL COUNCILS own blocks of flats such as the one shown above. Some council-run estates have problems such as drugs or crime and not everyone likes living there.

takes the child away from the parents and into care. Most children in **council care** are placed in a **children's home** until a more permanent solution can be found. Some return to their natural parents, while others are placed with **foster parents**. Some children are eventually **adopted**.

 ## Helping the elderly and disabled

The second group the council looks after consists of adults who may be old or have a disability. The council supports these people in their own homes, sending in **home helps** and supplying **meals-on-wheels**.

If a person cannot remain at home, the council will look after them in a home. **Social services** work closely with the **health authorities** and **doctors**.

Education

Until 1870, education in Britain was a luxury for most children rather than an entitlement for all. High-quality education had to be paid for, and was run by a mixture of religious and charitable institutions.

Every person from the age of five to sixteen has the right to free education, provided by the local council in primary and secondary schools.

State schools

Throughout most of Britain, the local council has overall responsibility for education through a **local education authority (LEA)**. In rural areas it is the **county council** that is responsible. Most children attend state-run schools.

Although schools are classified differently in different parts of the country, all are run by a **board of governors**. The board consists of the head teacher, parents, teachers, representatives of the local authority and members of the local community.

The local council sets the annual budget for each school and provides a range of **support services**. It also educates children who have been excluded from school and looks after those who have **special needs**, such as a disability or difficulties with reading. For those able to cope in a mainstream school, it provides extra help and support.

Outside school

Outside school, the local council runs **youth clubs** and other facilities, as well as **swimming pools** and **sports centres**. Councils also run free **public libraries**, where you can go to borrow a book or study. Many libraries now have computer facilities so that you can use the Internet or send e-mails to your friends.

LIBRARIES are also run by your local council. Here, children read books in a mobile library that travels from place to place.

LOCAL COUNCILS organise education in their areas, but schools, like this secondary school, are run by their governors.

Councils also run a range of **adult education classes**, often in partnership with a local college, so that adults can continue to learn and study when they have left school. There are English classes for those new to this country, and classes to help those unable to read or write. For very young children, councils run or support a range of **nursery** and play schools, providing a free place for every four-year-old child who requires it.

The role of the state

Although local authorities are involved with education, **national government** has the main role. It lays down the **curriculum** to be followed, and checks school standards and performance through OFSTED, the Office for Standards in Education. It sets the rate of teachers' pay, is responsible for teacher training and also manages post-16 education at colleges and universities.

Over the years, the balance between local and national control of education has shifted. Today, many responsibilities have been taken over by national government and by schools and school governors themselves. **Local education authorities** are now mainly responsible for providing the structure and framework of education, rather than providing the education itself.

The local council is run by a group of elected representatives known as councillors. Their job is to represent the views and interests of their constituents. Why do people do it, and who are they?

Why become a councillor?

People become **councillors** for a variety of reasons. Some stand to change their local community for the better; others stand because they have worked for a **political party** and want to represent that party on the council.

Who stands for election?

Councillors must be 21 or over and have lived within the council's boundary for the previous 12 months or be on its **electoral roll**; in addition, they must not work for the council they are standing for.

The number of councillors on a local council varies according to the size of the local population. The average number is 40 for a district council and 60 for a London borough, unitary authority or county council.

Each councillor represents an area known as a **ward**, which might have up to 12,000 electors in it. In most councils, each ward elects two or three councillors. Many rural councils and all county councils have one councillor per ward.

COUNCILLORS often attend local meetings, for example to decide whether a building development should go ahead.

Councillors can solve some problems with just a phone call or a letter, but other issues can take months of hard work to resolve.

A LOCAL COUNCILLOR'S diary is usually full of meetings.

The workload

Each councillor's workload is enormous. They must attend both **full council meetings** and meetings of any **committees** they sit on. Most of these meetings take place in the evening, to allow working councillors to attend, and might not finish until after 11 pm. In addition, they meet council officers to discuss current council issues. As a member of a political party, they also attend the **monthly group meeting**, as well as other political events.

Some councillors hold a senior position on the council, such as **leader**, or **chair** of an important committee like education. This extra responsibility means hours of work in meeting council officers, chairing committee meetings and fronting a council department as its elected head.

Meetings and visits

Beyond their work at the **town hall**, councillors attend meetings in their own wards, perhaps held by a tenants' association or residents' group. In addition, most councillors hold a regular, often weekly, **advice surgery** to which their constituents bring council-related problems.

Visits to constituents' homes are also common, particularly if the constituent is housebound. All councillors receive many phone calls and letters, asking their help in dealing with all kinds of problems.

Case work on behalf of constituents can be very time consuming – a hundred cases on the go at any one time is not unusual. In addition, action by a councillor to get something done in the ward can take hours of work. It is not surprising that councillors have little time for anything else.

The mayor

The mayor is one of the most visible members of the local council. Wearing the distinctive chain of office, he or she is often seen opening an event or attending a concert. But what does the mayor do?

Electing the mayor

The **mayor** is an **elected councillor** and usually comes from the ranks of the largest **political party**. In general, a mayor has served time as **deputy mayor** and is often one of the older council members, respected for his or her local knowledge and ability to get along with everyone.

The mayor is elected at the **annual general meeting** of the council at the end of May. He or she takes an **oath** of office, chooses a **deputy**, and is installed for a one-year **term**. Most local councils in urban areas have a mayor, or **Lord Mayor** if a city, but county councils and most district councils elect a chairperson instead. In Scotland, the same role is taken by the **Provost** or Lord Provost.

Unlike other mayors, Lord Mayors of London have a show every year, when they ride in a carriage.

What the mayor does

The mayor chairs the **full council meetings**, which take place five or six times a year. The mayor keeps order and makes sure business is conducted properly. The mayor does not participate in any **debate**, nor vote.

This largely ceremonial position becomes important if no **political party** has full control of the council; in this case, the mayor might be called upon to use a **casting vote** to decide an issue one way or other. This can bring the mayor into party politics.

MAYORS represent the council in public. Here the mayor of Haringey, wearing her chain of office, attends a community event.

The mayor's most important role is to represent the council at all public events. Inside the town hall the mayor greets visitors to the town and acts as official **host** at civic receptions. Outside, the mayor attends school speech days, opens new buildings, gives out prizes, visits old peoples' homes, meets members of the voluntary sector and generally acts as the public face of the council.

 ## A new role

In May 2000 the role of mayor began to change. For the first time in Britain Londoners had the chance to elect their mayor. Unlike other mayors, the **mayor of Greater London** is a hands-on politician and political leader, running the new **Greater London Authority** and controlling and directing many aspects of daily life in London.

Within a few years, other British cities, such as Liverpool, Birmingham and Cardiff are likely to elect their own mayors, changing the role of mayor from largely ceremonial to one of the most important and powerful political posts in Britain.

Election time is one of the most exciting times in the council's year. Candidates for office canvass for votes, people put up posters in their windows and volumes of literature are shoved through every letter box.

Candidates can come from all walks of life. However, many will be retired or in a part-time job since council work can take up many hours a week.

When elections take place

The date of a general election for Parliament varies, but the dates of **council elections** are fixed. They are always held on the first Thursday in May, with the exception of **by-elections** called to fill a vacancy, which can take place on any Thursday.

Elections for **councillors** in London, Northern Ireland and the county councils are held every four years; in Scotland and Wales, elections are held every three years.

Election timetable

Overall responsibility for running an election rests with the council's **returning officer**. During the year, the officer and his or her team draw up the **electoral roll** of those able to vote. When the election is called, he or she publicises the election, draws up the timetable and organises **polling stations** (places where people vote) in each ward.

While council officials organise the election, the **candidates** set to work. Each candidate must be nominated by ten ward electors and can appoint an **agent** to deal with all the official paperwork. The candidates **canvass** for votes by telephone or by knocking on front doors and introducing themselves, wearing a large coloured **rosette** to identify their political party.

POLLING STATIONS, where people cast their votes, are often schools or community centres converted for election day.

Election day

On **election day, candidates** tour their **ward** to show a high profile and encourage people to vote for them. Party workers sit outside **polling stations** taking the **electoral numbers** of voters to check that those who promised their support have voted.

Later in the day candidates and workers visit those who have not voted, offering to take them to the polling station as encouragement. Inside the polling station the election officers issue **ballot papers** and help people if they have problems.

The count

After the **polls** close at 9pm, the candidates and their supporters go to the town hall. Here votes are counted by council officers and other workers. When the **count** is complete, the **returning officer** announces the result. New councillors are elected, ready to serve their term.

It costs a lot of money to run a local council. A small rural council can easily spend £20 million a year, while large cities such as Birmingham or Glasgow spend well over £1,500 million a year.

WHERE THE COUNCIL'S MONEY COMES FROM

Charges for parking, council housing, leisure services

National government grant

Council tax and rates

Where the money comes from

Local authority **finance** is one of the most complex areas of local government. The rules and regulations are precise and detailed, and all local authorities employ large numbers of **accountants** to keep track of their money. Independent local government **auditors** check to make sure it is spent legally and efficiently. Some parts of the budget are **ring-fenced** (kept separate) from others, that is, the money earned from one service can only be spent on that service, and not on any other.

In very rough figures, about one third to one half of council income comes from charges.

Charges and rents

A large portion of council **income** comes from **charges**. These charges include **rent** from council houses, **fines** from illegal parking, **fees** for planning permission, and so on. But this still leaves a huge gap.

To fill this, national government gives numerous **grants** to local authorities. These grants are paid for out of national taxation and include specific grants for housing, education and social services. In addition there is a large general grant, the **revenue support grant**, which tops up the individual grants. Together, these grants account for about another third of a council's income.

The remaining third of a council's income comes from two sources in roughly equal amounts. The first is **non-domestic** or **business rates**. These rates are collected by the local council, paid into a national pool and distributed to each local council on the basis of its population.

Council tax

The final source of income is the **council tax**. This local tax is paid by the owner or tenant of every property and varies according to the value of the property. All properties are placed in one of eight bands, ranging from Band A (properties worth up to £40,000) to Band H (properties over £320,000).

The different bands are set in relation to Band D, which is known as the **headline rate**. Across the country, the Band D rate varies from under £400 to over £1,000. Council tax gets a lot of attention since it is the only part of a local council's income which comes directly from local taxation. Yet it is one of the smallest sources of a local council's income.

Making decisions

During the course of a year, a council makes many thousands of decisions. Some are hugely important and affect many people, such as the level of next year's council tax.

Councils are responsible for vast sums of money and must make sure that they spend it wisely.

A complex process

The theory of local government states that councillors decide, and **officers** carry out those decisions. In practice, the process is more complex.

Councillors drawn from the majority political party on the council, or from two or more parties working together in a **coalition**, form an **administration**. At the annual general meeting, the **majority party** nominates a leader and deputy leader, chairs of committees and sub-committees.

Once all the nominations have been made there is a vote, and the people who will hold the posts are **confirmed** by the full council. Councillors sit on each committee in proportion to the number of seats their party has on the council.

Proposals for action

At each committee meeting, councillors consider **papers** written by council officers proposing a course of action. These proposals have been discussed and agreed with the **chair** of the committee beforehand, and so in most cases will be agreed by the **majority** of the committee and become **council policy**. **Opposition councillors** can move **amendments**, and the committee might decide to accept them. When the issue is finally agreed, council officers carry out the decisions.

TO INFLUENCE council decisions, people fill in questionnaires, sign petitions, write letters and let their local councillors know their views.

Carrying out decisions

Council officers range from part-time secretaries and receptionists to the **chief executive**. They work according to national law, government directives and the decisions made by councillors. However, the day-to-day implementation of these instructions is in their hands, so in practice they have considerable freedom of action.

How you can affect decisions

How can you affect or influence these decisions? Almost all **committee meetings** are open to the public, and you can attend them. Sometimes you will be allowed to speak. To make sure your views are known well in advance, write, phone or visit your local councillor at one of their regular **surgeries** to lobby them to support your view.

To get publicity for your views, write to your local newspaper, or contact your local radio station to find out if they are interested. You can also draw up a **petition** for people to sign.

Councillors are elected and need votes to survive. They therefore listen closely to what their constituents have to say, even if they don't agree with them. They know that if they disagree too often, they can be voted out of office.

How to complain

In an ideal world your local council would run all its services efficiently and effectively so that you would have no cause to complain. But councils can make mistakes, or take decisions you think are wrong.

IF A COUNCIL gets something wrong, you can complain in person, by writing letters, or, once you have tried other channels, through the ombudsman.

Getting the message across

One of the major problems facing local councils is letting people know what they are doing. Councils print their own newspapers and leaflets, but not everyone will see or read such information. Many people are therefore surprised when the council acts in a certain way, and complain.

'I'd like to complain...'

What should anyone who has a **complaint** do? The first step is to ring or write to your local council. If you do not know the name of the council officer responsible, write to the **chief executive** of the council or to the **head** of the relevant department. All councils undertake to reply to a letter within a stated period – usually 10 to 14 days.

Each department of the council usually has a **complaints officer** who monitors the progress of complaints. A **central complaints officer** deals with major complaints. It is important to complain if something has gone wrong so the council can make sure that the mistake is not repeated.

If you are still unhappy, you can contact your **local councillor** and get them to raise the issue on your behalf, or you can contact your local paper or radio station to make them aware of the issue. If neither of these work, complain to the local **ombudsman**.

It is your right to complain if the council gets something wrong, because it is your money that is paying for it.

The **Commission for Local Administration** (England, Scotland and Wales have separate commissions) is appointed by the government to investigate complaints against councils. The commissioners, known as **ombudsmen**, only consider cases that have already gone through the council's complaint machinery; cases can be referred directly by the person complaining or through a **local councillor**.

If the ombudsman thinks that the council has a case to answer, she or he examines it and issues a report. The report might find the council at fault and suggest how the council could rectify the matter. The council is obliged to consider the report, but does not have to agree to its recommendations. In practice, however, most councils agree to all the recommendations.

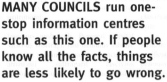

MANY COUNCILS run one-stop information centres such as this one. If people know all the facts, things are less likely to go wrong.

There are as many different systems of local government around the world as there are countries, for each country has devised its own. Here is a brief look at two very different systems.

IN FRANCE, local government can be _really_ local – 11,000 out of more than 36,000 _communes_ have a population of less than 200.

France

France is a very **centralised** country, with power concentrated in the government in Paris. The most important local government figure used to be the **prefect**, appointed by the Ministry of the Interior in Paris for every local **_commune_** (community), **department** and **region**, to keep a tight control over local affairs. In recent years, moves have been made to give power to the regions.

France is divided into 22 regions, in which there are 96 sub-regions. Below them are local communes, ranging in size from the smallest village to the cities of Paris (which is divided into 20 **_arrondissements_** or boroughs), Marseilles and Lyon.

Every six years voters in each commune elect their councillors, who in turn elect the mayor. The mayor is an important local figure, acting both as political leader of the council and, in the bigger towns, as chief executive of the council's administration.

The USA

Unlike France, the USA has always had strong local government. Each of the 50 states is **self-governing** and each one organises local government in a different way with different names and responsibilities for each council.

IN THE USA, counties vary in size from a few hundred people to the 3.5 million citizens of Los Angeles. The average size is 80,000.

A US citizen might vote in presidential, congressional, state, county, municipal, one or more special district, school board, and perhaps even local township elections.

The basic unit is the **county**, of which there are about 3,000. These counties contain 35,000 cities, boroughs and townships, in which there can also be local district councils.

In addition, there are another 18,000 cross-boundary **special district councils** looking after particular services, such as irrigation or sewage, and about 34,500 **cross-boundary school boards** looking after education. In total, the USA has more than 90,000 local councils, or one for every 3,000 people: the ratio in Britain is one council for every 125,000 people.

The most important figure in local government is the **directly elected mayor.** Mayors of huge cities such as New York or Los Angeles have enormous personal power. City councillors hold the mayor and senior officers to account for their actions and can pass **ordinances** (local laws) which the mayor can agree to or reject.

There are two drawbacks to the local government system in the USA: every council is directly elected, and all their boundaries and many of their responsibilities overlap. A US citizen might therefore vote in at least eight overlapping levels of government as opposed to the two to four in Britain.

budget
The annual calculation of how much money a council earns and therefore how much it has to spend. The total budget determines the level of the council tax and the quantity and quality of services offered.

business rates
Business or non-domestic rates levied on business properties. The rate is collected by the local council, paid into a national pool and then distributed to each local council on the basis of its population.

canvass
To seek a person's vote and support in an election.

capital spending
The money a council spends on buildings and other long-term assets, as opposed to revenue spending.

constituent
Someone who lives in a councillor's ward.

council
The elected organisation that runs local services in your area. Today there are four main types of local council in Britain: county, unitary, district and parish.

council tax
A local property tax levied on home owners and tenants to help pay for the council's services.

councillor
An elected member of the council.

democracy
A system of government by the people or their elected representatives.

elector
A person on the electoral roll who is able to vote in council elections.

foster parents
Parents who look after a child on behalf of the local council, usually for a short period.

full council

The regular meeting of all councillors chaired by the mayor. Full council meetings usually take place five or six times a year.

grant

A sum of money given for a particular purpose. The national government gives grants to local councils to pay for specific and general services.

health authority

The organisation responsible for the provision of health services in a region. Health authorities fund local hospitals, doctors, health visitors and other services.

local education authority

The borough, district, city or county council responsible for education in your area.

local government

The lowest level of government in this country, consisting of local councils.

ombudsman

The Commissioner for Local Administration who handles complaints of maladministration or injustice brought by members of the public against a local council.

parish

The smallest unit of local government, based on the ancient boundaries of the local Anglican church.

revenue spending

Money spent on day-to-day council services, including staff salaries and short-term items, such as electricity or printing. Revenue spending is financed by government grants, business rates, council tax and charges.

ring-fenced

Money raised by a service which can only be spent on the same service. For example, rents from council housing are ring-fenced and can only be used for repairs and other housing-related services, not for education or roads.

unitary authority

A local authority responsible for all services. In other parts of the country, service delivery is split between county and district councils.

ward

The geographical area represented by a councillor. Most councils have 20 or so wards.

PICTURE CREDITS
Cover image: Franklin Watts
(Chris Fairclough)
Format pp. 1, (Sally Lancaster),
3 (Joanne O'Brien), 5 (Mo Wilson),
10 (Sally Lancaster),
13 (Paula Glassman), 15 top
(Joanne O'Brien), 15 bottom (Lisa
Woolcett), 16 (Paula Solloway),
19 (Brenda Prince), 21 (Mo
Wilson), 27 (Joanne O'Brien)
Marketing Manchester © p. 6